Grandma Hands in the Pot

Dr. Gloria M. Milow

Cover design by Scribe Freelance Book Design, Co.
Interior design by Scribe Freelance Book Design, Co.

MG's Publishing
1415 Highway 85N Ste. 310-430
Fayetteville, Georgia 30214

www.mgspublishing.com
www.facebook.com/MGsPublishing1
www.instagram.com/mgspublishing
www.twitter.com/MGsPublishing
$Dr Gloria Milow via CashApp

ISBN: 978-0-9793537-3-4
Library of Congress Control Number: 2021918600

Dedication

To my grandchildren: Quincy M. Johnson, Jaylin Johnson, Capri Pierce, Princess Milan Johnson, Kaylee Fields, Jada M. Johnson, Seven Y. Johnson, Zen Marrie, Sydney Johnson, and to my great grandchildren and generations to come!

Acknowledgments

My mother, "Momma" Elease Milow Nelson, grandmother "Mo Mo" Martha Woods Greene, grandmother "Ma Bessie" Bessie Alexander Milow, great grandmother "Ma Ma" Elizabeth Nevilles Woods, and great grandfather Hosea Alexander, Sr.

Sweet babies, this book is for you. I desired to open up "The Pork House." As of this day, I have not opened it but I want to leave my legacy to all of you just in case you need to know how to fix something delicious to eat that I once cooked in my life.

Mo Mo made delicious T cakes (cookies), popcorn balls, pecan candy, ice cream, and the best fried chicken. She did a lot of preserves (fig, strawberry, pears, peppers). She made small sweet potato pies, covered with crust all around. She worked in the kitchen as a cook in Opelousas, Louisiana at "The Palace Cafe." She made tripe fia'. It was delicious.

Ma Ma (Mo Mo's Mother) made the best fried chicken and fried fish with sweet potato fries.

I loved Ma Bessie's crawfish bisque, étouffée, boiled shrimp and crabs. She had the best fried chicken. She made the best pastries. We would always have desert with a glass of milk.

Grand Pa Hosea (Ma Bessie's daddy) raised all of his children after the death of his wife Sally Alexander. He cooked, clothed and sheltered them all by himself... He was a very gentle man that smoked a pipe. He knew how to cook everything. He made the best rum cakes. He made great baked chicken, beef tips, BBQ sauce, BBQ chicken, smothered steaks, gumbo, etc. He had so many good dishes.

Because each of our tastes are different, I will tell you the ingredients to use in each dish, but you are allowed to put any amount you want accordingly.

Recipes for Your Family

Seven's Collard Greens, page 11

3   Dedication

4   Acknowledgments

11   Seven's Collard Greens

Da Prince's Cabbage with Carrots

Empress' Cool Garden Salad

June June's Potato Salad

12   Lisa's Stir & Fry

Sharon's Grilled Stir Fry Lobster

Elizabeth's Beet Salad

Mo Mo's Cheesy Okra Casserole

15   Princess' Smothered Louisiana Goulash

K K's Squash

Da Prince's Broccoli Mixed with Shrimp, page 15

Da Prince's Broccoli and Shrimp

Seven's Chili Cheese Fries with Jalapeño

16   Bessie's BBQ Pigs Feet

Me Me's Peas and Carrots

Jada's Spinach Dip

Grand Pa Hosea's Turkey Meatballs with Green Beans

19   Saul's Oyster Giblet Dressing

Momma's Fried Chicken

Ma Ma's Smothered Chicken, Buttered Carrots and Salad with Homemade Pickles

20   Monica's Chicken Salad

Zen Marrie's Smothered Steak with Dirty Rice

23   Mike Ala's Grilled Lobster

Elease's Beef Enchiladas

GrandPa's Boiled Shrimp

24   Seven's Crab Pot

June June's Boiled Crab, Lobster, Cucumber Salad, and Baked Potato with Spinach Dip

27   Marie's Shrimp Scampi

Princess' Grilled Salmon

LaSha's Fried Catfish

28   Ma & Doe Peski's Fried Oysters, Shrimp Fries and Tomato Cucumber Salad

Quincy's Seafood Gumbo with Garlic Toast

31 Sululah's Salmon Croquette

Marie's Brown Rice

Ma Bessie's Tuna Salad

Martha's Smoked Turkey Wings

32 Lee's Turkey Spaghetti

Jada's Turkey Burritos

Bob's Tacos

35 Mike's Turkey Stuffed Bell Peppers

Mike's Grilled Pork Chops

Sharon's Smothered Pork Chops with Cream Potatoes

36 Piccola Ribs

Mesha's Cheesy Grits

Gee Gee's Smothered Potatoes

39 Milan's Scrambled Eggs, Rice, and Bacon

Momma G's Stuffed Angel Eggs

Mo Mo's Mac 'n Cheese

40 Ma Bessie's Glazed Strawberries

Momma G's Cheesy Mashed Potatoes

43 About the Author

Seven's Collard Greens

Da Prince's Cabbage with Carrots

Empress' Cool Garden Salad

June June's Potato Salad

Seven's Collard Greens

2 tablespoons grapeseed oil

1 lb. collard greens, shredded

½ teaspoon Cajun seasoning

a pinch brown sugar

1 onion, chopped

2 garlic cloves, chopped

1 can of mushroom soup

HEAT the grapeseed oil on medium heat. Add all ingredients and seasoning. Stir frequently for about 20 – 25 minutes.

Da Prince's Cabbage with Carrots

1 tablespoon unsalted butter

1 onion, chopped

1 head of cabbage, shredded

3 large fresh carrots, sliced

1 tablespoon grapeseed oil

½ tablespoon honey

1 can of mushroom soup

1 teaspoon pepper

1 teaspoon Cajun seasoning

HEAT the butter with onions in a skillet, then place the cabbage and carrots into the skillet. Pour the grapeseed oil on it. Cover skillet and stir occasionally for 25 minutes.

Empress' Cool Garden Salad

1 head lettuce

2 tomatoes

1 cucumber

1 small bag of carrots

WASH and cut all the vegetables. Use your choice of salad dressing.

June June's Potato Salad

1 lb. potatoes

3 eggs, boiled

2 tablespoons relish

3 tablespoons mayonnaise

½ teaspoon Cajun seasoning

1 onion, chopped

2 green onions

1 tablespoon mustard

½ teaspoon garlic powder

WASH, dice and drain the potatoes. Add all the ingredients together in a bowl. Cut the white of the boiled egg into pieces and mash the yolk up. Mix well.

Lisa's Stir & Fry

Fresh or frozen vegetables will work.

2 tablespoons avocado oil

1 lb. carrots

1 lb. broccoli

1 lb. portabella mushrooms

1 onion

1 tablespoon honey

½ teaspoon Cajun seasoning

1 tablespoon garlic powder

HEAT the skillet on medium. Coat with avocado oil and mix all ingredients. Cook for 20 minutes.

Sharon's Grilled Stir Fry Lobster

2 tablespoons garlic oil

2 Vidalia onions, chopped

1 green bell pepper, chopped

1 orange bell pepper, chopped

1 bunch cilantro, chopped

1 bunch green onions, chopped

1 lb. lobster tails, chopped

1 tablespoon garlic powder

1 teaspoon black pepper

1 teaspoon thyme

1 pinch brown sugar

HEAT the garlic oil and onions on the grill/stove top. Stir fry until the heat becomes medium hot. Add the other ingredients on the grill. Stir fry for 20 minutes and serve over brown rice.

Elizabeth's Beet Salad

2 cans pickled beets, sliced

1 tablespoon apple cider vinegar

2 tablespoons mayonaise

1 pinch brown sugar

½ cup Vidalia onions, chopped

MIX everything together in a bowl. Chill for about 15 minutes.

Mo Mo's Cheesy Okra Casserole

3 tablespoons grapeseed oil

1 lb. okra (fresh or frozen)

1 lb. corn (fresh or frozen)

3 tomatoes (fresh)

1 tablespoon Cajun seasoning

2 garlic cloves, chopped

2 onions, chopped

2 eggs

1 cup shredded cheese

HEAT oil until hot. Place okra in the pot, stirring until all the slime is out.

Lisa's Stir & Fry

Sharon's Grilled Stir Fry Lobster

Elizabeth's Beet Salad

Mo Mo's Cheesy Okra Casserole

Princess'
Smothered
Louisiana
Goulash

Da Prince's
Broccoli
and
Shrimp

K K's
Squash

Seven's
Chili
Cheese
Fries with
Jalapeño

ADD the corn, tomatoes, seasoning, and seasoning. Mix well. Add both eggs. Stir well and place the shredded cheese in. Put everything in the oven for 25 minutes.

Princess' Smothered Louisiana Goulash

1 lb. okra (fresh or frozen)

1 lb. corn (fresh or frozen)

3 tablespoons grapeseed oil

1 teaspoon garlic powder

1 lb. clean shrimp

1 lb. smoked sausage

2 fresh tomatoes

1 tablespoon Cajun seasoning

SAUTÉ the chicken in a pot with unsalted butter. In another pot, sauté ½ chopped onions.

K K's Squash

1 zucchini squash, sliced

1 banana squash, sliced

2 tablespoons grapeseed oil

½ tablespoon garlic powder

½ teaspoon black pepper

½ teaspoon Cajun seasoning

MIX everything in a pan and cover with foil.

Grill for 10 – 15 minutes.

Da Prince's Broccoli and Shrimp

1 lb. broccoli, cut

1 lb. large shrimp

2 teaspoons garlic oil

1 onion, chopped

2 tablespoons grapeseed oil

WASH and sauté the shrimp in the garlic oil on medium. Sauté the onion and broccoli in another skillet of warm grapeseed oil. When it becomes tender (about 10 minutes), add the shrimp. Cook for 10 – 15 minutes.

Seven's Chili Cheese Fries with Jalapeño

1 lb. potatoes, sliced

avacado oil

1 teaspoon Cajun seasoning

1 can chili

1 cup shredded cheese

2 tablespoons sour cream

1 jalapeño pepper, sliced

1 tablespoon onion, chopped

FRY the potatoes in hot avocado oil until medium brown. Add the Cajun seasoning. Drain the oil from the potatoes.

ADD chili and the fried potatoes in a warm pot. Sprinkle the shredded cheese over the chili and fries. Drop the sour cream, some jalapeño pepper slices, and the chopped onions on top.

Bessie's BBQ Pigs Feet

12 pigs feet, cut in half

2 tablespoons garlic seasoning

bay leaves

2 bell peppers, diced

2 onions

2 bottles of BBQ sauce

3 garlic cloves, minced

BOIL the pigs feet in all the other ingredients (except BBQ sauce) until tender.

PLACE the feet in an oven pan. Add BBQ sauce on top and cook at 350 degrees for 30 – 40 minutes.

Me Me's Peas and Carrots

1 lb. peas and carrots (fresh or frozen)

1 cup water

a pinch of brown sugar

½ teaspoon unsalted butter

½ teaspoon Cajun seasoning

½ teaspoon grapeseed oil

BRING water to a boil. Place the oil, seasoning and sugar in the pot. When it starts boiling again, place the peas and carrots on medium heat for 10 – 15 minutes.

Jada's Spinach Dip

1 lb. organic spinach

1 lb. unsalted butter

1 lb. gouda cheese

1 lb. Parmesan cheese

1 lb. Philadelphia cream cheese

1 pint heavy cream

OVER medium fire, heat the heavy cream, melt the butter, add the cheeses, stir frequently and add the spinach. Cook for 10 – 15 minutes.

Grand Pa Hosea's Turkey Meatballs with Green Beans

1 lb. ground turkey

1 lb. green beans (fresh or frozen)

1 chopped onion

1 tablespoon grapeseed oil

1 tablespoon Cajun seasoning

½ teaspoon garlic powder

Me Me's Peas and Carrots

Bessie's BBQ Pigs Feet

Jada's Spinach Dip

Grand Pa Hosea's
Turkey Meatballs

Saul's Oyster Giblet Dressing

Ma Ma's Smothered
Chicken, Buttered
Carrots and Salad with
Homemade Pickles

Momma's Fried Chicken

SEASON the ground turkey and roll into little round balls. Pre-cook them in the grapeseed oil.

REMOVE them from the pot. Season and cook the green beans in the rest of the grapeseed oil for about 10 minutes.

ADD the meat balls until its a simmering gravy, about 10 minutes. Makes a quick, scrumptious meal over rice.

Saul's Oyster Giblet Dressing

1 loaf cornbread (preferably homemade)

1 chopped onion

2 stalks celery

½ teaspoon thyme

1 teaspoon avocado dressing

2 raw eggs

3 jars oysters

1 stick unsalted butter

½ cup milk

SAUTÉ raw oysters in unsalted butter and 1/2 cup of onions.

MIX all ingredients (except milk and cornbread) in a bowl using your hands. Pour in milk and place all ingredients in an oven pan for 30 – 35 minutes. Serve with cornbread.

Momma's Fried Chicken

1 tablespoon Cajun seasoning

1 tablespoon garlic powder

1 cup all-purpose flour

4 eggs

1 chicken

hot sauce, to taste

½ cups of either olive oil, avocado oil or grape-seed oil

WASH the chicken thoroughly, and sauté it with hot sauce.

IN another bowl, sprinkle the seasoning in the flour.

CRACK the eggs into a separate bowl and whisk.

DIP the chicken in the eggs. Flour and fry the chicken in the oil of your choice. Turn your chicken over and cover the skillet so it can cook thoroughly.

Ma Ma's Smothered Chicken, Buttered Carrots and Salad with Homemade Pickles

½ tablespoon Cajun seasoning

½ tablespoon garlic powder

2 tablespoons all-purpose flour

½ cup onions, chopped

½ cup green pepper, chopped

½ cup water

1 chicken

1 small bag carrots

1 cup chicken broth

2 teaspoons butter

½ teaspoon honey

3 slices tomatoes

3 pieces of lettuce, shredded

pickles (preferably homemade)

BOIL the carrots in the chicken broth.

WASH the chicken and season it. Coat with all-purpose flour.

PLACE the chicken in a medium-hot pot and turn it over when browned. Add onions, green pepper, and water. Cover and stir frequently for 20 minutes.

Monica's Chicken Salad

2 16oz chicken chunks (cooked) or 1 broiled chicken, chopped

1 teaspoon Cajun seasoning

½ teaspoon garlic powder

1 chopped onion

2 tablespoons mayonnaise

1 tablespoon sweet relish

2 green onions, chopped

2 boiled eggs, peeled (the white chopped and the yolk mashed)

1 small can of tuna

SEASON the chicken with Cajun and garlic powder.

MIX the chopped chicken in a bowl with the rest of the ingredients above for 10 minutes.

Zen Marrie's Smothered Steak with Dirty Rice

1 steak

½ teaspoon Cajun seasoning

½ teaspoon garlic powder

½ teaspoon pepper

avacado oil

1 cup rice

1 lb. ground turkey

1 chopped onion

1 green bell pepper, sliced

1 tablespoon avacado oil

1 bottle steak sauce

2 eggs

COAT the steak with all-purpose flour, Cajun, garlic powder, and pepper.

PLACE the seasoned steak in a medium-hot pot of avocado oil. Cook for 5 minutes on each side.

Monica's Chicken Salad

Zen Marrie's Smothered
Steak with Dirty Rice

Grilled Lobster

Beef Enchiladas

Boiled Shrimp

Mike Ala's Grilled Lobster

1 lb. lobster tails

½ teaspoon thyme

1 tablespoon garlic powder

1 tablespoon Cajun seasoning

1 onion, chopped

1 orange bell pepper, chopped

2 green onions, chopped

½ lb. salted butter

HEAT the grill with the butter on medium heat. Add all the ingredients. It's ready to eat in 15 minutes with a delicious salad.

Elease's Beef Enchiladas

12 tortillas

1 tablespoon avocado oil

1 lb. shredded cheese

1 can of black olives, chopped

1 lb. ground beef (pork, chicken, or just cheese will also work in this recipe.)

1 onion, chopped

1 bunch of cilantro, washed and cut thinly

3 green onions, chopped

1 tablespoon Cajun seasoning

1 tablespoon garlic powder

2 tablespoons Gebhardt chili powder

HEAT the tortillas in avacado oil.

SEASON the meat with Cajun, garlic, chili powder, onion, cilantro, and green onions.

WRAP the cheese, olives, and meat and roll the tortilla and place it in the pan. Heat in the oven for 10 minutes.

GrandPa's Boiled Shrimp

2 lbs. large shrimp

4 lbs. crabs

1 large bottle bay leaves

1 bag Zatarain's Creole Boil

1 whole onion

2 lemons

3 tablespoons garlic powder

PLACE 5 cups of water into a pot. Heat the water until it boils.

ADD all the ingredients in the pot until the crabs and shrimp are cooked (about 30 minutes).

Seven's Crab Pot

You can use any amount of the ingredients without measurements.

water

lemon

2 onions

Zatarain's Crab Boil

sausage

potatoes

turkey necks or neck bones or chicken

crabs

shrimp

corn

½ tablespoon pepper

1 tablespoon Cajun seasoning

3 tablespoons garlic powder

1 small bag bay leaves

1 tablespoon bay seasoning

BOIL water with all ingredients. Cook for 40 – 45 minutes.

June June's Boiled Crab, Lobster, Cucumber Salad, and Baked Potato with Spinach Dip

4 lobster tails

3 lbs. crab

1 small bag bay leaves

½ teaspoon black pepper

1 tablespoon Cajun seasoning

2 tablespoons garlic powder

1 large baked potato

1 cup hot butter

1 small bag spinach

1 cucumber, sliced

½ teaspoon apple cider vinegar

1 tablespoon mayonnaise

BOIL lobster and crab in a pot of boiling hot water with bay leaves, black pepper, Cajun seasoning, and garlic powder. Cook for 30 – 35 minutes.

MICROWAVE the potato for 8 minutes. Cut the potato in half and add 1 tablespoon of butter.

HEAT the spinach in hot boiling water and drain. Pour the spinach over the potato.

ADD the apple cider vinegar and mayonnaise to the cucumber slices. This is a great full dinner.

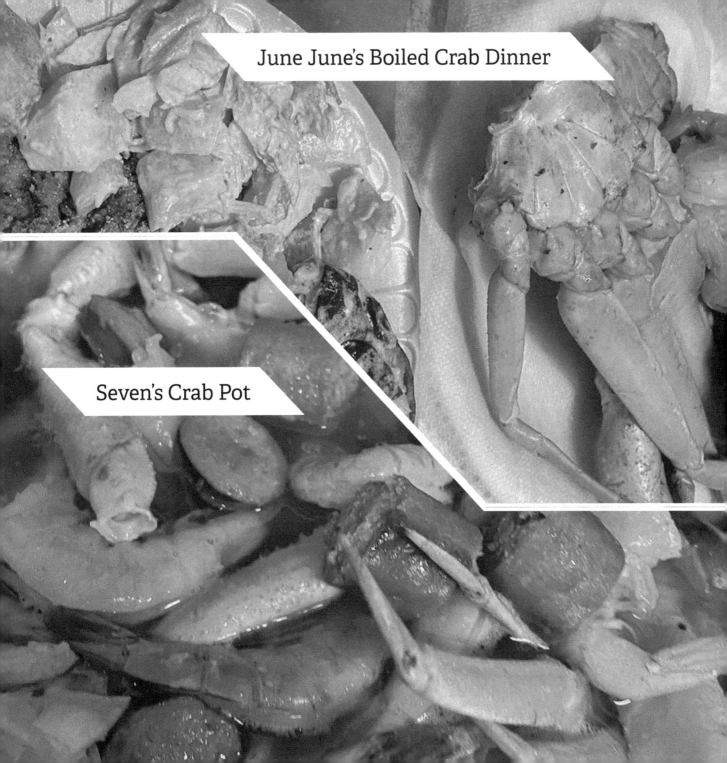

June June's Boiled Crab Dinner

Seven's Crab Pot

Marie's Shrimp Scampi

Princess' Grilled Salmon

La Sha's Fried Catfish

Marie's Shrimp Scampi

2 cloves garlic, chopped

1 lemon, sliced

2 tablespoons grapeseed oil

½ cup onions, chopped

2 scallions, chopped

1 lb. clean large shrimp

½ teaspoon garlic powder

½ tablespoon black pepper

2 tablespoons unsalted butter

SOAK the garlic and lemon overnight.

HEAT the oil in the pot. Sauté the shrimp.

ADD the onions and scallions into the pot, along with the sautéed shrimp, seasoning, and unsalted butter.

COOK for 15 minutes.

Princess' Grilled Salmon

2 lbs. salmon

3 lemons, sliced

2 onions, chopped

½ tablespoon garlic butter

½ tablespoon garlic powder

½ tablespoon Cajun seasoning

WASH the salmon. Season and butter. Grill the salmon with the lemons and onions for 20 minutes.

LaSha's Fried Catfish

1 fresh catfish

½ teaspoon Cajun seasoning

½ teaspoon garlic powder

1 lb. yellow cornmeal

1 cup olive oil

HEAT the skillet on medium.

SEASON and shake the seasoned catfish in some yellow cornmeal.

PLACE the fish in the hot olive oil for 7 minutes on each side.

Ma & Doe Peski's Fried Oysters, Shrimp Fries and Tomato Cucumber Salad

1 jar raw oysters

1 lb. large clean shrimp

2 bags yellow cornmeal

1 cup olive oil

½ teaspoon Cajun seasoning

½ teaspoon garlic powder

SEASON the oysters and shrimp.

SHAKE the oysters in a bag of yellow cornmeal. Do the same with the shrimp.

HEAT olive oil in a medium hot skillet and fry the oysters for 5 – 10 minutes.

FRY the shrimp in the hot grease for 7 ½ minutes on each side.

Quincy's Seafood Gumbo with Garlic Toast

1 tablespoon butter

1 garlic, chopped

1 lb. turkey necks

3 lbs. crabs

1 lb. clean large shrimp

6 bay leaves

3 tablespoons garlic powder

½ cup crab boil

2 tablespoons grapeseed oil

1 garlic toast

2 lbs. chicken breast

ADD the butter to a skillet, and cook the garlic in it. Put the skillet in the oven and leave it for 20 seconds.

COOK the turkey necks until tender.

ADD the crabs and shrimp last. Put them in a large pot with about 5 cups of water, and add the bay leaves, garlic powder, crab boil, and grapeseed oil. Cook for about 45 minutes.

POUR 4 cups of water into a large pot. Boil the chicken.

SERVE with the garlic toast.

Quincy's Seafood Gumbo

Fried Oysters, Shrimp and Salad

Sululah's Salmon Croquette

Marie's Brown Rice

Ma Bessie's Tuna Salad

Martha's Smoked Turkey Wings

Sululah's Salmon Croquette

1 salmon, fresh or canned

1 onion

1 bell pepper

½ teaspoon garlic power

½ teaspoon Cajun seasoning

1 egg

flour to coat

½ cup olive oil

ADD the salmon, onion, bell pepper, seasonings, egg, and some flour in a bowl and mix.

POUR oil in a frying pan. When it's hot, pat the salmon in patties and fry them on both sides.

Marie's Brown Rice

1 cup water

1 teaspoon avocado oil

1 teaspoon salt

½ cup rice

BOIL the water and add avacado oil to it. Add the salt and rice, simmer over the fire and cover the pot until done. (The water should be fully evaporated, and there should be holes in the rice when it is ready.)

Ma Bessie's Tuna Salad

1 can of tuna

2 boiled eggs

½ teaspoon Cajun seasoning

1 tablespoon mayonnaise

1 teaspoon relish

½ cup chopped onion

MIX all the ingredients together in a bowl and you have a delicious tuna salad.

Martha's Smoked Turkey Wings

turkey wings

2 cups water

2 tablespoons Cajun seasoning

½ cup black pepper

½ teaspoon thyme

1 cup onions, chopped

1 tablespoon Worcestershire sauce

3 chopped garlic cloves

an aluminum pan

PUT all the ingredients in an aluminum pan. Cover the pan and bake for 40 – 45 minutes on 350 degrees until they are tender and golden brown.

Lee's Turkey Spaghetti

½ tablespoon salt

1 tablespoon garlic oil

1 box of spaghetti

1 lb. ground turkey

1 cup onions, chopped

3 cloves garlic

1 tablespoon Cajun seasoning

1 bottle chili powder

1 jar of mushroom pasta sauce

1 cup shredded cheese

BOIL 1 cup of water. Add salt and garlic oil to it. When the water is boiling, add the pasta to it and follow the instructions on the box.

PLACE the ground turkey in a medium pot.

ADD the onions, garlic and seasoning in the pot and stir often.

DRAIN the pasta and mix it with the ground turkey and place the mushroom sauce in the pot. Stir and pour into a pan with the grated cheese. Bake for 15 – 20 minutes.

Jada's Turkey Burritos

1 pack ground turkey

1 bottle Gebhardt chili powder

½ teaspoon garlic powder

½ teaspoon Cajun seasoning

1 cup onions

1 pack flour tortilla (12 count)

1 lb. shredded cheese

1 pint sour cream

1 bunch cilantro, chopped

COOK the ground turkey with the seasoning and onions.

WARM the tortilla and fill it with the turkey, 1 tablespoon of cheese, a teaspoon of sour cream and 1 teaspoon of cilantro. Wrap the tortilla and set aside. Repeat for the next tortillas.

Bob's Tacos

1 lb. ground beef or ground turkey

1 cup green onions

½ teaspoon Cajun seasoning

½ teaspoon garlic powder

1 bunch cilantro

1 cup onions, chopped

2 tablespoons grapeseed oil

12 corn tortillas

Lee's Turkey Spaghetti

Jada's Turkey Burritos

Bob's Tacos

Mike's Turkey Stuffed
Bell Peppers

Mike's Grilled Pork Chops

Sharon's Smothered
Pork Chops with
Cream Potatoes

1 tablespoon Gebhardt chili powder

2 cups lettuce, shredded

2 tomatoes, thinly sliced

1 cup shredded cheese

1 pint sour cream

1 jar salsa

SEASON and cook the meat in grapeseed oil.

HEAT the tortillas—one at a time—and add the rest of the ingredients to each "taco shell." Use some salsa as garnish and enjoy your taco!

Mike's Turkey Stuffed Bell Peppers

3 large green bell peppers

1 – 2 lbs. ground turkey

½ tablespoon Cajun seasoning

½ tablespoon garlic powder

3 cups shredded cheese

SLICE the bell peppers in half. Fill a pan with a layer of water (enough to coat the bottom of the pan, but not enough to let water get into the peppers), and place the peppers in the pan.

SEASON the turkey and cook it. Fill each bell pepper with turkey and 2 tablespoons of cheese.

BAKE for 30 minutes, makes a great meal.

Mike's Grilled Pork Chops

7 center cut pork chops

1 tablespoon garlic powder

1 tablespoon Cajun seasoning

FIRE up the grill. When the coals mellow down, season and put in the pork chops.

Sharon's Smothered Pork Chops with Cream Potatoes

center cut pork chops

½ teaspoon pepper

1 tablespoon garlic powder

1 tablespoon Cajun seasoning

2 tablespoons avocado oil

1 tablespoon flour

1 onion, chopped

1 bell pepper, chopped

4 potatoes

½ teaspoon unsalted butter

½ cup milk

½ teaspoon garlic powder

WASH center cut pork chops. Season with pepper, garlic, and Cajun.

HEAT 1 tablespoon oil on medium. Flour the meat with ½ tablespoon flour. Place in the hot oil until each side is brown. Remove from pan and drain the excess oil.

CLEAN your skillet. Pour the remaining avocado oil in the skillet on medium heat, along with the remaining flour, ½ cup onions and bell pepper. Keep stirring the pot until it turns medium-brown. Add the pork chops and cook for about 10 minutes.

BOIL the potatoes, then drain them. Add the butter, milk, and garlic powder. Mash together and serve with the pork chops.

Piccola Ribs

4 ribs

1 tablespoon pepper

1 tablespoon garlic powder

1 tablespoon liquid smoke

1 onion, chopped

1 bell pepper, sliced

WASH and season ribs with pepper, garlic, and liquid smoke.

PLACE the meat on a medium hot grill and watch the meat for about 40 minutes.

Mesha's Cheesy Grits

1 teaspoon salt

¼ cup grits

1 cup shredded cheese (optional)

1 teaspoon butter

BOIL 1 cup of water and add salt to it. When the water starts to boil, add the grits. While the grits boil, add the cheese and stir until it is all melted. When serving the grits, put 1 teaspoon of butter on top.

Gee Gee's Smothered Potatoes

6 medium potatoes, diced

salt

Cajun

2 tablespoons garlic powder

½ teaspoon black pepper

2 tablespoons grapeseed oil

butter

1 onion, chopped

scallions, chopped

salt pork

PEEL the potatoes and season with the salt, Cajun, garlic, and pepper. Pour grapeseed oil into a medium hot skillet. When the oil is hot, pour the potatoes into the skillet. Stir the potatoes so they will not stick nor burn. When the potatoes are tender, serve them with butter.

Piccola Ribs

Gee Gee's Smothered Potatoes

Mesha's Cheesy Grits

Milan's Scrambled Eggs, Rice, and Bacon

Mo Mo's Mac 'n Cheese

Momma G's Stuffed Angel Eggs

BOIL the salt pork until tender. Cut them and fry in some hot grapeseed oil. Remove from the pan and drain the excess oil from the salt pork. Serve the salt pork with the potatoes for a mouthwatering breakfast.

Milan's Scrambled Eggs, Rice, and Bacon

½ teaspoon unsalted butter

2 eggs

½ teaspoon salt

½ teaspoon garlic powder

1 cup rice

½ teaspoon shredded cheese

2 slices bacon

MELT the butter over medium heat. Whisk the eggs and season them. Scramble the eggs for 3 minutes.

BOIL 2 cups of water with salt and unsalted butter. Add the rice. When the rice cooks down, put the lid on the pot until fluffy.

PUT the bacon in a skillet and fry on each side until it's crispy (about 3 minutes).

Momma G's Stuffed Angel Eggs

a dozen eggs

½ teaspoon garlic powder

½ teaspoon relish

1 tablespoon mayonnaise

½ teaspoon pepper

BOIL all the eggs until hard-boiled, about 10 minutes.

CUT the eggs in half.

REMOVE the yolk, mash and season.

MIX in a bowl and stuff the egg whites with the seasoned yolk.

Mo Mo's Mac 'n Cheese

½ teaspoon salt

1 tablespoon olive oil

1 lb. bag macaroni pasta

1 pint sour cream

1 cup milk

3 eggs

16oz bag shredded cheese

1 jar of Cheez Whiz, melted

½ teaspoon Cajun seasoning

½ teaspoon garlic powder

1 stick unsalted butter

BOIL 4 cups of water and add the salt and the oil to it.

ADD the pasta and follow the instructions on the box to cook.

DRAIN the pasta.

MIX all of the ingredients in a bowl (including the hot pasta). Grease a pan and pour in the mac 'n cheese. Bake for about 20 minutes.

Ma Bessie's Glazed Strawberries

2 lbs. bag strawberries, frozen

½ pack brown sugar

3 tablespoons honey

WASH the strawberries and cut them how you like.

ADD honey or brown sugar to your liking.

Momma G's Cheesy Mashed Potatoes

4 potatoes

½ teaspoon garlic butter

1 cup shredded cheese

1 tablespoon unsalted butter

½ cup milk

WASH and peel the potatoes.

BOIL 2 cups of water with the garlic butter.

PLACE the potatoes in the water and let them boil until they are tender. Drain.

MASH with the cheese, butter, and milk. Ready to serve!

Ma Bessie's Glazed Strawberries

Momma G's Cheesy Mashed Potatoes

About the Author

D r. Gloria M. Milow, a native of New Orleans, is the founder and pastor of MG's Full Gospel Church. She has a Doctorate of Philosophy in Pastoral Ministry and 45 years of experience teaching and counseling, four of those years as an assistant principal. Dr. Milow has been a guest on various local and syndicated media outlets, including the "Pimps in the Pulpit" segment of The Michael Baisden Show. She is also a motivational speaker and the founder of the Healn' Hurtn' Women. She was a guest of KJLH in 2019. She was a nominee for the Best High School Teacher Award and for Steve Harvey's 2009 – 2011 Hoodie Award. Author, publisher, and very proud grandmother of King Quincy, and three grandbaby dolls of Atlanta.

CPSIA information can be obtained
at www.ICGtesting.com
Printed in the USA
BVHW061035291121
622781BV00010B/430